EP
Earth Science
Printables:
Levels 5-8

This book belongs to:

_____

This book was made for your convenience. It is available for printing from the Easy Peasy All-in-One Homeschool website. It contains all of the printables from Easy Peasy's earth science course. The instructions for each page are found in the online course.

Easy Peasy All-in-One Homeschool is a free online homeschool curriculum providing high quality education for children around the globe. It provides complete courses for preschool through high school graduation. For EP's curriculum visit allinonehomeschool.com.

EP Earth Science Printables: Levels 5-8

ISBN: 9798568666318

First Edition: December 2020

Physical Map

On the map below, label 5 mountain ranges and 5 rivers. Color the desert areas yellow.

https://d-maps.com/carte.php?num_car=3271&lang=en

My Rock

Fill in this worksheet on your rock. Draw a picture of it in the box.

Color: _____

Texture: _____

Weight: _____ (heavy/light)

Luster: _____

Hardness: _____

Streak: _____

Cleavage: _____

My Rock

Fill in this worksheet on your rock. Draw a picture of it in the box.

Color: _____

Texture: _____

Weight: _____ (heavy/light)

Luster: _____

Hardness: _____

Streak: _____

Cleavage: _____

My Rock

Fill in this worksheet on your rock. Draw a picture of it in the box.

Color: _____

Texture: _____

Weight: _____ (heavy/light)

Luster: _____

Hardness: _____

Streak: _____

Cleavage: _____

Rock Types

Fill in this chart about different kinds of rocks.

Types of Rock	How it looks/feels	How it's used	Why it's used for this
Chalk			
Clay			
Granite			
Marble			
Pumice			
Sandstone			
Slate			

Earth Science
Levels 5-8

(This page left intentionally blank)

Earth Science
Levels 5-8

Mineral Crystals

Cut on the solid lines, fold on the dotted lines. Assemble the various mineral crystal shapes. This is a rhombic prism. Minerals with this shape include topaz, sulfur, and barite.

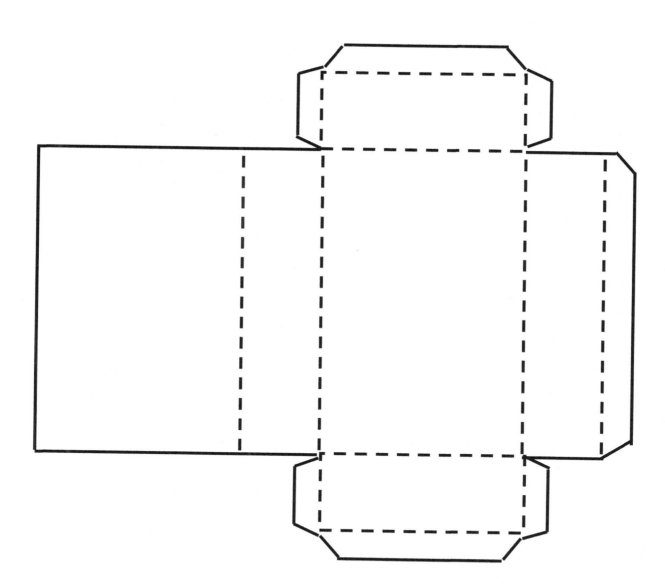

Earth Science
Levels 5-8

(This page left intentionally blank)

Mineral Crystals

Cut on the solid lines, fold on the dotted lines. This is a tetragonal dipyramid. Zircon is an example of a mineral with this shape.

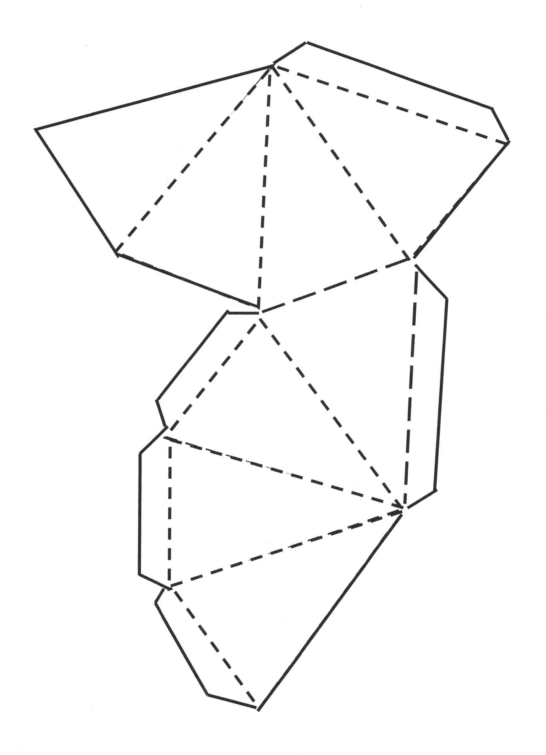

Mineral Crystals

Cut on the solid lines, fold on the dotted lines. This is a cube. Salt is a mineral with this shape.

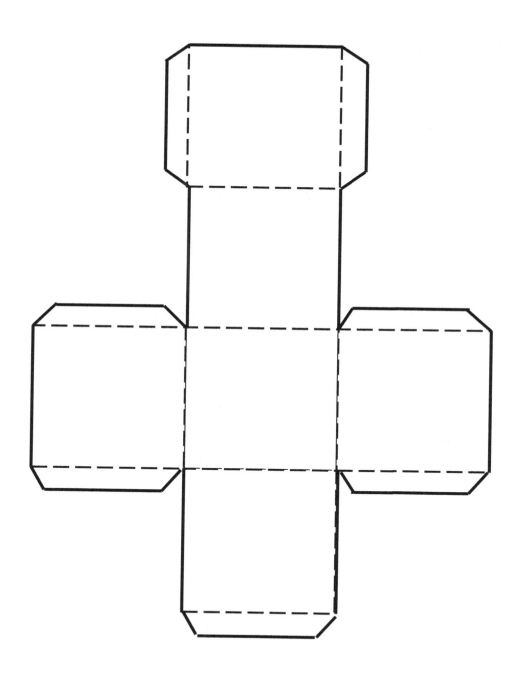

(This page left intentionally blank)

Mineral Crystals

Cut around the outside of the entire shape, keeping the tabs attached. Fold on the dotted lines and use the tabs to glue the shape together. This is a hexagonal quartz.

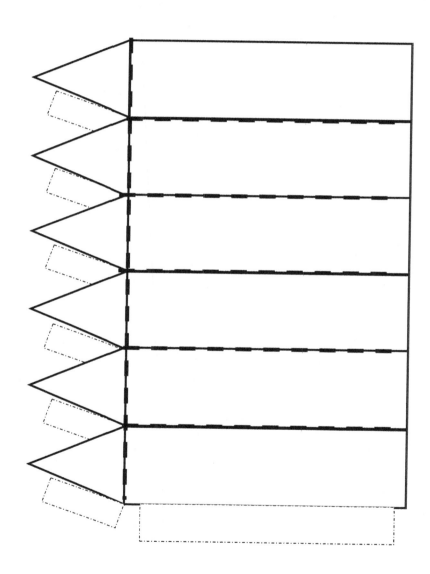

(This page left intentionally blank)

Cloud Finder

Cut around the outside of the first circle, as well as along the dotted lines to cut out the "cut out here" section. Cut around the outside of the second circle. Stack the first circle on the second circle and secure with a brad. Can you find today's clouds on your cloud finder?

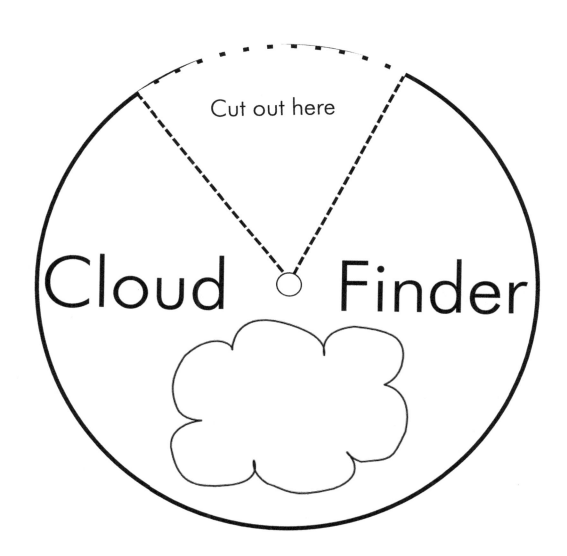

Earth Science
Levels 5-8

(This page left intentionally blank)

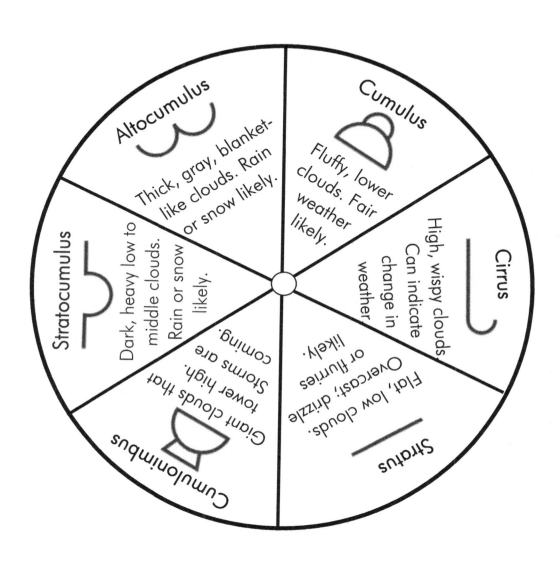

(This page left intentionally blank)

Earth Science
Levels 5-8

Cloud and Weather Chart

Use your cloud finder to predict the weather. Leave the last spot blank until later in the day.

Date/ Time	Cloud Type	AM Weather	Predicted Weather	Weather/ Time

Precipitation Map

Color the map using the maps linked in the online course to help. Be sure to include a key!

Global Wind Patterns

Draw on the global wind patterns from your reading today.

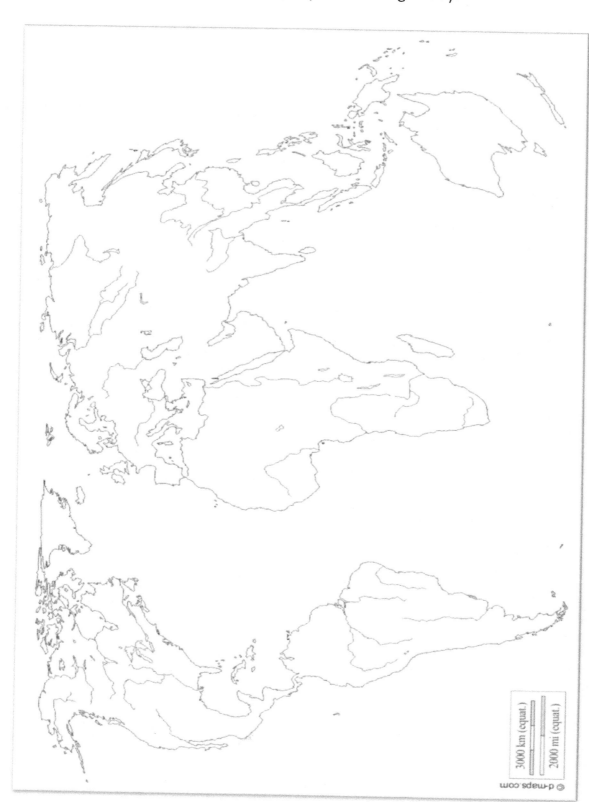

3000 km (equat.)

2000 mi (equat.)

© d-maps.com

https://d-maps.com/carte.php?num_car=3271&lang=en

Weather Chart

Use this chart for the next five days, following the instructions in the online course.

Date	Temp	Conditions	Wind	Dew Point	Humidity	Barometric Pressure

Midwest

Choose the map that contains your state. Follow the directions in the online course to make a weather map. You'll need four of the same map.

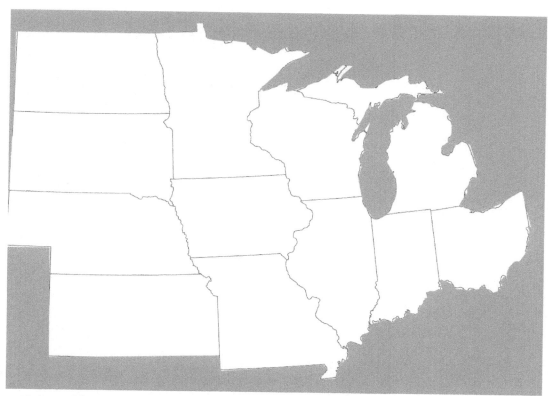

Adapted from: https://freevectormaps.com/united-states/US-EPS-01-1002?ref=atr

Midwest

Adapted from: https://freevectormaps.com/united-states/US-EPS-01-1002?ref=atr

Midwest

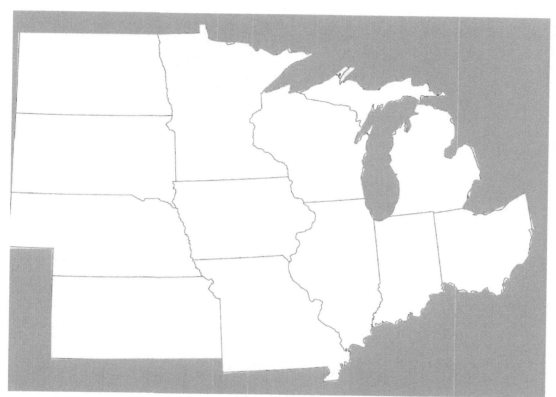

Adapted from: https://freevectormaps.com/united-states/US-EPS-01-1002?ref=atr

Midwest

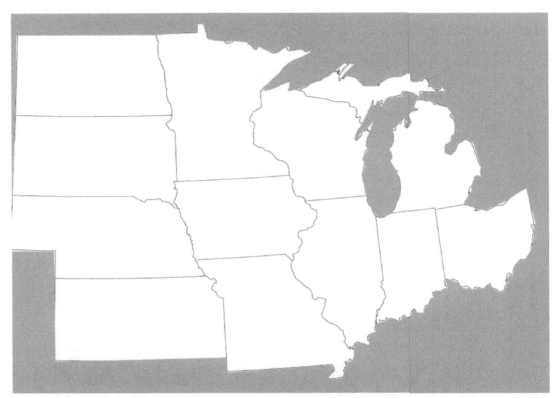

Adapted from: https://freevectormaps.com/united-states/US-EPS-01-1002?ref=atr

Northeast

Choose the map that contains your state. Follow the directions in the online course to make a weather map. You'll need four of the same map.

Adapted from: https://freevectormaps.com/united-states/US-EPS-01-1002?ref=atr

Northeast

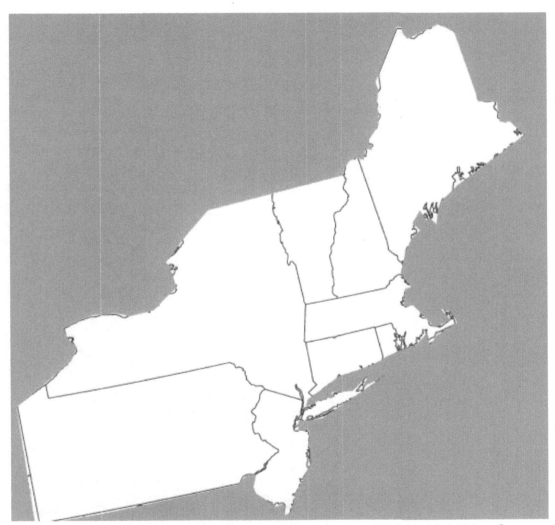

Adapted from: https://freevectormaps.com/united-states/US-EPS-01-1002?ref=atr

Northeast

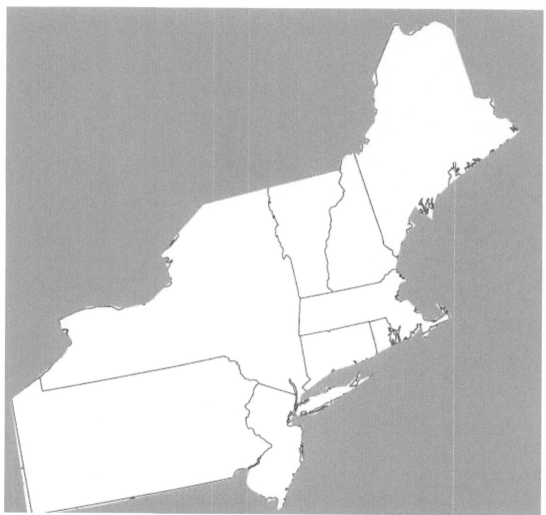

Adapted from: https://freevectormaps.com/united-states/US-EPS-01-1002?ref=atr

Northeast

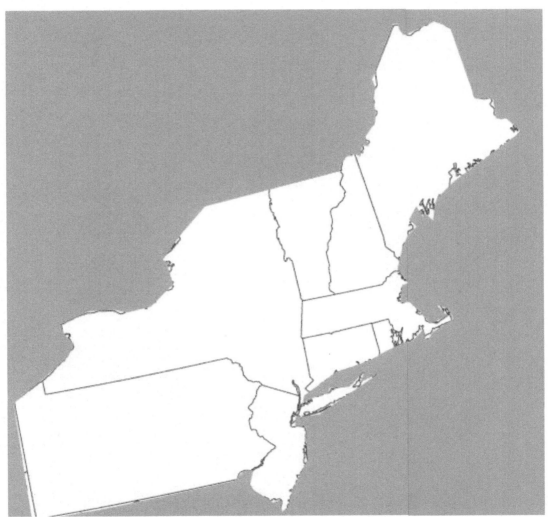

Adapted from: https://freevectormaps.com/united-states/US-EPS-01-1002?ref=atr

South

Choose the map that contains your state. Follow the directions in the online course to make a weather map. You'll need four of the same map.

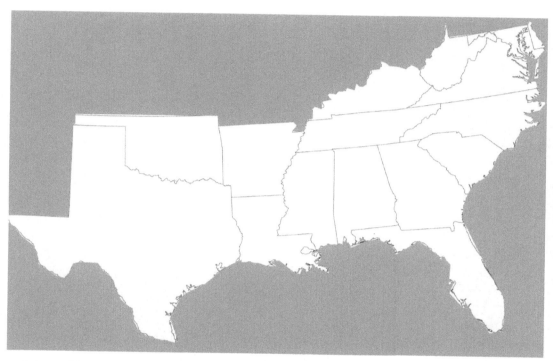

Adapted from: https://freevectormaps.com/united-states/US-EPS-01-1002?ref=atr

South

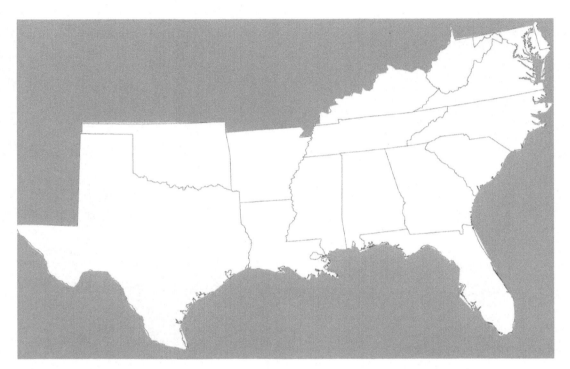

Adapted from: https://freevectormaps.com/united-states/US-EPS-01-1002?ref=atr

South

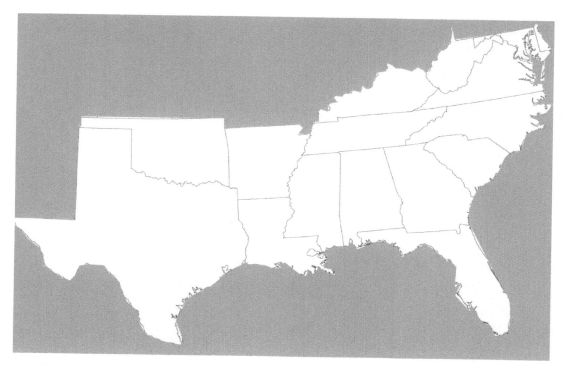

Adapted from: https://freevectormaps.com/united-states/US-EPS-01-1002?ref=atr

South

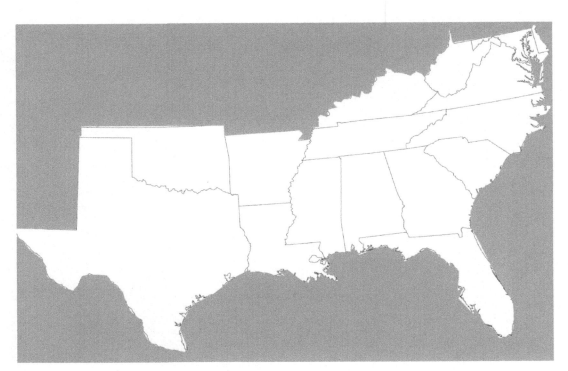

Adapted from: https://freevectormaps.com/united-states/US-EPS-01-1002?ref=atr

West

Choose the map that contains your state. Follow the directions in the online course to make a weather map. You'll need four of the same map.

Adapted from: https://freevectormaps.com/united-states/US-EPS-01-1002?ref=atr

West

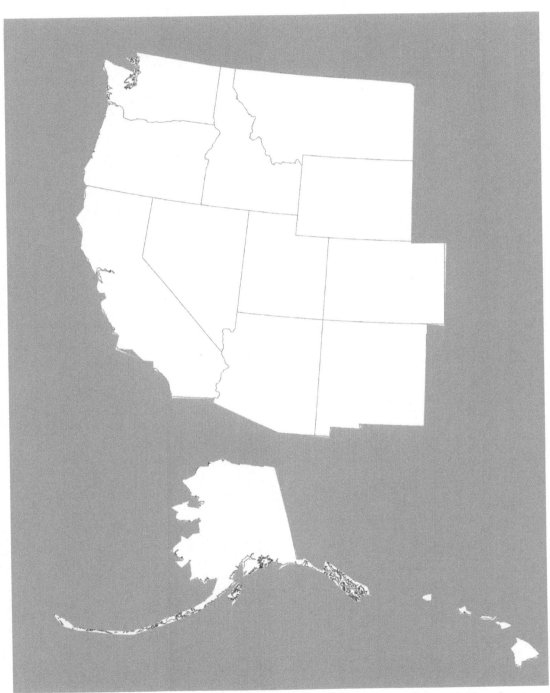

West

West

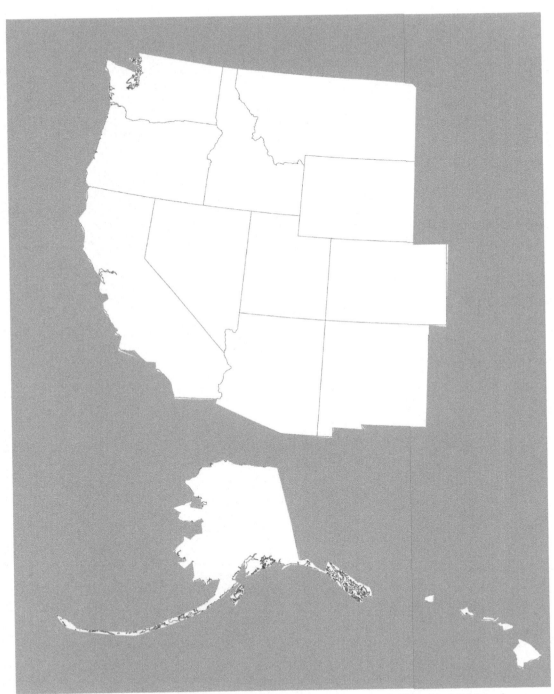

Mapping

Draw the rivers on the map following the instructions in the online course.

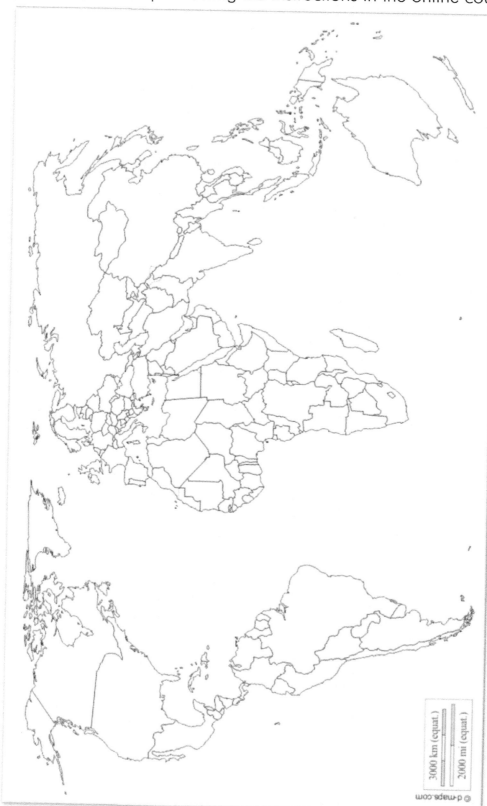

https://d-maps.com/carte.php?num_car=13181&lang

(This page left intentionally blank)

Oceans Lapbook

Cut out as one piece. Fold the flaps so that the words are on the cover. Write the answers inside.

Why is the Ocean Blue?

Why is the Ocean Salty?

(This page left intentionally blank)

Ocean Lapbook

Cut the top rectangle out as one piece. Fold matchbook style. Write the answers inside.

What Causes Waves?

Earth Science
Levels 5-8

(This page left intentionally blank)

Ocean Lapbook

Cut out both circles. Label one circle "Atlantic Ocean" and one "Pacific Ocean." Treat each circle like a pie graph and color in the approximate percentage of the world's sea water that ocean represents using the online information. You can cut out the title banner to glue in your lapbook above or below the circles.

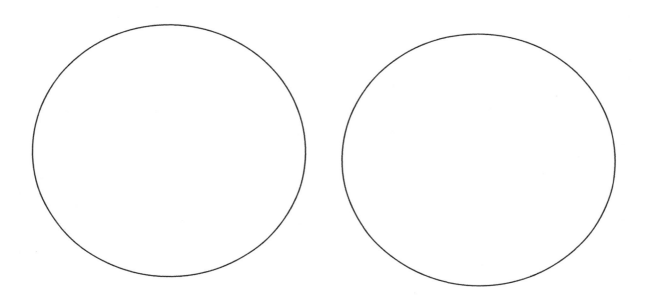

Percentage of the world's sea water

(This page left intentionally blank)

Earth Science
Levels 5-8

Ocean Lapbook

Cut out as one piece. Fold in half and crease well. Cut on the two black lines separating the words to make three flaps. Simply fill in one thing in each from the website or search for some more info on your own.

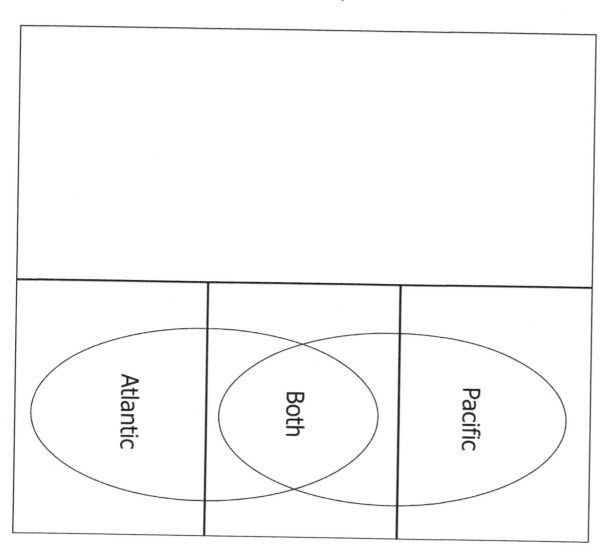

(This page left intentionally blank)

Ocean Lapbook

The piece on the right gets stacked on top of the wider one of the same height. This is the Neritic piece. These other three get stacked on top of all the other pieces, fattest to skinniest.

Neritic

Splash Zone

Intertidal

Subtidal

Cut out each rectangle on the black lines and stack as described on the next page.

Aphotic

Pelagic

Earth Science
Levels 5-8

(This page left intentionally blank)

Ocean Lapbook

Oceanic

Cut out each rectangle on the black lines.

Euphotic

Stack with the others with the shortest in front. Then the three from the other page go in front. Make a cover out of sand colored paper (if possible). Cut it to look like the descending land in the diagram. Staple all together. Older students can write about each one. Use the Light Zones page. Younger students can color the levels darker and darker instead of writing on them. This piece goes with the "Zonation" page of the site.

Disphotic

(This page left intentionally blank)

Ocean Lapbook

Use the instructions online to complete this piece.

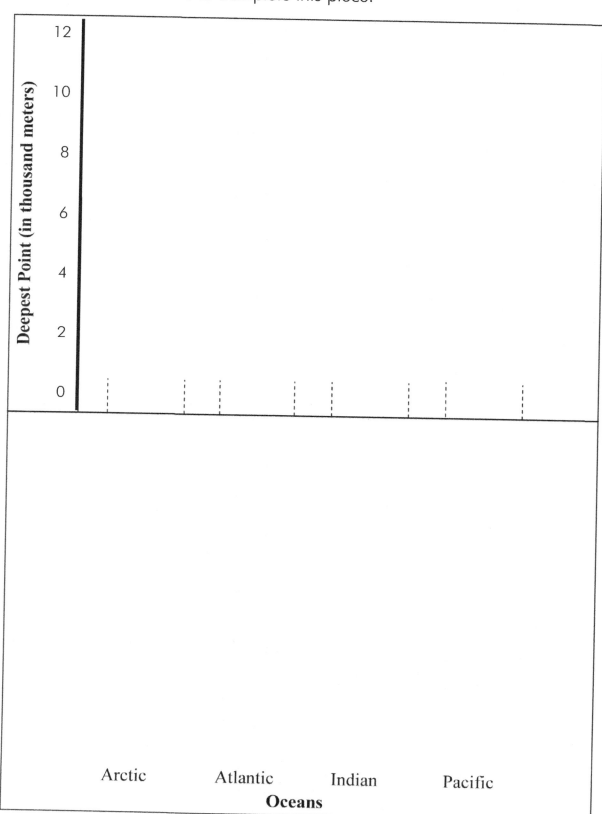

(This page left intentionally blank)

How Deep is the Ocean?

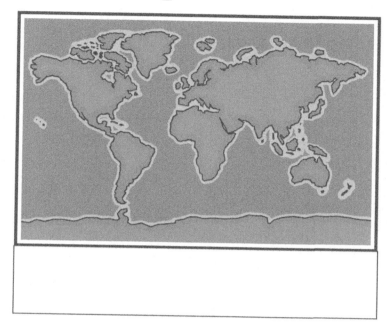

Earth Science
Levels 5-8

(This page left intentionally blank)

Ocean Lapbook

The Ocean Refreshes Itself

Cut the rectangle above as one piece. Keep on the tabs. Cut along the dotted lines.

Fold the tabs back and glue them down. You will also put glue on the back of these tabs to attach it to the lapbook.

Cut out the skinny rectangles along the black lines.

Insert the "cold water" strip to the left so that it pulls down.

Insert the "water flows" strip to the right so that it pulls up.

In the blue sections you could use the info in the other animated diagram on the webpage to write "Organic…"

When you attach to the lapbook, only glue down the sides and middle.

Sinks

Cold
water

Water flows
toward the
equator

Pushing
water up to
the surface

Earth Science
Levels 5-8

(This page left intentionally blank)

Ocean Lapbook

Cut out as one piece and fold the side flaps into the middle so that the words and picture are on the outside. Write facts about kelp inside.

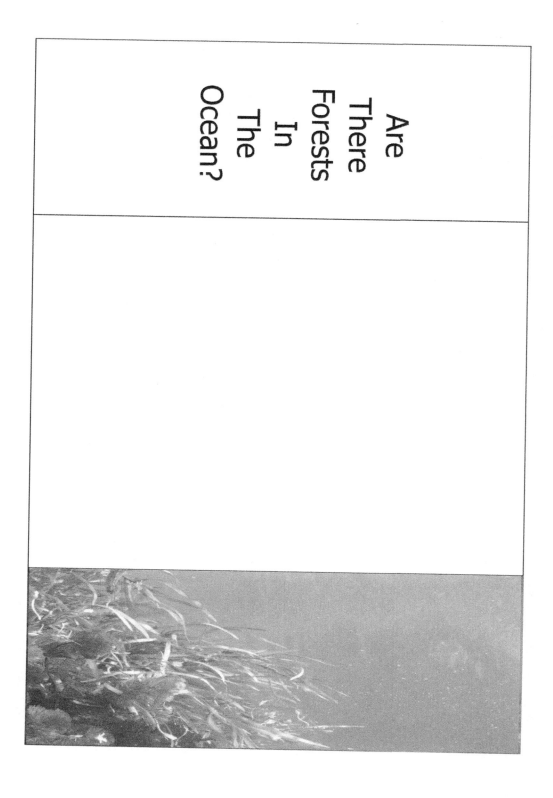

(This page left intentionally blank)

Big Dipper

Find the big dipper in this picture. If you want to, take this page outside tonight and use it to try to find the Big Dipper in the sky.

Research Notes

Use these pages to make notes on your topic.

Topic:_____

Resource 1:_____

Info:_____   Info:_____

Info:_____   Info:_____

Info:_____   Info:_____

Resource 2:_____

Info:_____   Info:_____

Info:_____   Info:_____

Info:_____   Info:_____

Resource 3:_____

Info:_____   Info:_____

Info:_____   Info:_____

Info:_____   Info:_____

Resource 4:_____

Info:_____   Info:_____

Info:_____   Info:_____

Info:_____   Info:_____

Resource 5:_____

Info:_____   Info:_____

Info:_____   Info:_____

Info:_____   Info:_____

Resource 6:_____

Info:_____   Info:_____

Info:_____   Info:_____

Info:_____   Info:_____

Resource 7:_____

Info:_____   Info:_____

Info:_____   Info:_____

Info:_____   Info:_____

Resource 8:_____

Info:_____   Info:_____

Info:_____   Info:_____

Info:_____   Info:_____

Resource 9:_____

Info:_____   Info:_____

Info:_____   Info:_____

Info:_____   Info:_____

Made in the USA
Middletown, DE
25 August 2022

72308147R00038